The aim of

Sense & visualise the cosmic inf...
Palmistry & F....ᵤ .....

Palmistry is an art of palm reading and *Feng Shui* is an art of placement. These are well-proven arts and positive cosmic influences, which are and have been practised successfully over hundreds of years and have brought about a difference to ones lifestyle.

The two are inter-related in that *Palmistry* gives " **a sense of guidance**" and *Feng Shui* gives the "**direction (visualise)**" of one's life.

Who would not like to be a self motivated and a confident person? EVERYONE! – as this creates opportunity for success.

However, this can only be achieved if the *guidance* and *direction* are present in one's self. By inter-relating the two powerful positive energies of Palmistry and Feng Shui, I would like to show you in the simplest way, how to **Understand**, **Improve** and **Enhance** your life, and create opportunities in your **Career, Business, Relationship, Health, and Prosperity.**

ACKNOWLEDGMENTS

I wish to express my special thanks and gratitude to the people who made this book possible with their presence in my life. Firstly, to my late father Champaklal J. Parekh from whom I have been blessed with a special talent of hand reading. Secondly, to my dear husband and children who believed in me and encouraged me one hundred percent with their patience and generosity in allowing me to pursue my love for Palmistry and Feng Shui.

I hope that this book gives you as much enjoyment and fun as I have had in writing it.

Thank you.

CONTENTS

FOREWORD   Page

INTRODUCING PALMISTRY

THE HAND

CONTENTS

LINES   Page

FENG SHUI

CONTENTS

LINES

PALMISTRY

What is palmistry?

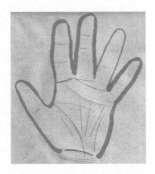

Palmistry is an ancient method of character analysis, whereby the shape, size, and colour of hands, clarity, length, position of the palm lines, are used to determine human personality and fate.

Hand reading is not a superstition, it actually portraits one's health, character and psychological state. Palmistry also known as - Chiromancy pronounced "kheir" - a Greek word meaning the hand, is an ancient method of character analysis, which dates to the prehistoric society approx. 15,000 years ago, it has certainly been known to have been practised over 5,000 years ago, by the ancient Greeks, Romans, Egyptians,

namely Aristotle, Hippocrates, Julius Caesar etc…

The main lines on our hands never change but do show any natural or hereditary dispositions that might have been acquired through the genes.

The appearance of the minor lines are the direct result of our psychological state and therefore, these minor lines change regularly according to our emotions and surroundings.

Psychologists have spent years researching the human minds little knowing that the hands are perfect mirrors of our minds which reveal what we are and not what we may pretend to be.

HOW PALMISTRY CAN HELP

Reading our own palm from time to time and looking out for special markings (please see the chapter on "Markings found on Mounts" and "Markings found on Lines") we can read our emotions, which sometimes we tend to ignore, or delay in dealing with it until its too late. We can use palm reading as a photographic feeling plates which acts as imprints of our own ideas, actions and decisions (whether they be consciously or unconsciously) which can have implications upon our lives.

By studying our hands and constantly monitoring our own markings, we may not be able to change our fate, but we can at least prepare ourselves for the warning to be taken as a challenge, and deduce, how to approach, and deal with the situation.

THE RELATIONSHIP OF PALMISTRY IN MEDICINE

In medicine, Palmistry is now being recognised as a powerful diagnostic tool. Cancer, Alcoholism and Heart Disease even in children in its earliest stages, can be detected through the knowledge of hand reading. Further diagnostic of ailments can be made through the nails, and hand markings, identifying causes of anxiety, and depression. Therefore, one can say that hand reading acts as a stethoscope and microscope for the very experienced palmist.

Although we cannot change our fate, by recognising this information we can diagnose and try to improve and utilise the information, in the best possible way.

Our fingertips are the most sensitive part of the hand which are protected by nails and therefore, nails are excellent indicators of health. Since it takes about 6 months for the nail to grow from the cuticle to the part where the nail is still embedded to the skin, one can detect what health or emotional problems have been experienced in the last 6 months.

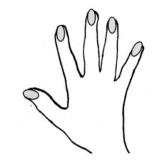

Nails come in all shapes and sizes and the main thing to look out for is the colour. A healthy colour should be slightly pale pink with white moon. Moons are inherited and will indicate any predisposition to any ailments or nutritional imbalance depending on their size.

FINGER PRINTS

Finger prints - also known as Palmer Skin pattern, was first researched by a young Czechoslovakian physician called Dr Jan Evangelista, in the early nineteenth century. He noticed that each fingerprint pattern is unique, and the right hand finger prints were not an exact copy of the left. Today, New Scotland Yard store approximately 5 million finger prints and the FBI store over 70 million, on their records. Finger prints are also extensively used by the Police to help them track down criminals.

PATTERN CHARACTERISTICS

loops   *peacocks eye*   *arch*   *tented arch*   *composite*

whorl

GENERAL CHARACTERISTICS

Loops - *flexible, confident and likes to keep busy*

Peacocks eye - *lucky, near misses from danger*

Arch - *industrious yet reserved & materialistic*

Tented arch - *enthusiastic and impulsive*

Composite - *indecisive but can see both sides of the problem or argument.*

whorl - *stubborn, strongly held view and prefers working alone*

WHICH HAND TO USE LEFT OR RIGHT?

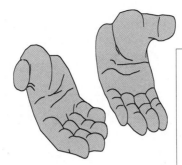

RIGHT (left side of the brain) deals with logic i.e.: reading writing calculation

LEFT (right side of the brain) i.e: deals with persona, health & progression

The left hand - your passive hand is believed to represent your inherent talents (unconscious self, imagination, reactions, natural aptitude and potential abilities) and holds information about childhood years and inherited health.

The right hand - or the dominant hand shows how one is developing (conscious self) giving information about events in our lives and our health.

Please note that the above applies to a right handed person and for a left handed person the rules are simply reversed.

DIVISION OF THE PALM

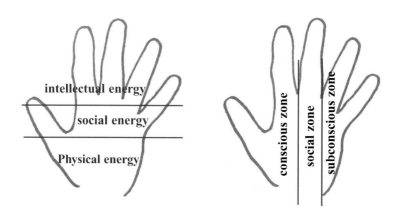

By studying the palm we can determine which part of the character has a greater emphasis.

The vertical   divisions emphasise the difference between the rational instinctive side of our personality (the thumb represents the ego), our conscious or rational self.   The other half represents our subconscious or instinctive side of our personality.

The horizontal division represents our vital energy, physical strength and robustness (shows love for life) which is emphasised on a well developed palm. Whereas an over developed palm suggests the individual is stubborn, a daredevil, and aggressive.

THE GENERAL CHARACTERISTICS OF THE SHAPE OF THE HAND AND FINGERS

CONIC: smooth fingers (absence of knots betweens the joints of the fingers) and with conic fingertips.

Character: takes things and others for granted whilst judging people at their face value. They can be easily distracted from duty and seek only the finer things in life but they are also very enthusiastic.

PHILOSOPHIC: long bony fingers and well developed joints (also known as knotty fingers). The Greek word 'philos' means love and 'sophia' meaning wisdom.

Character: egotistic and fanatical with analytical minds forever eager to learn. Their beliefs are from their own experiences in life via their own experiments. Apart from being secretive they are also cautious when choosing their words.

PSYCHIC: small, smooth and narrow fingers with pointed tips. Of all the types of hands this is the most attractive shape.

Character: loves to live in an idealistic world who has only a limited understanding of the real world which can only be appreciated by a similar type of hand. The owners of this shaped hand may find it difficult to be understood by others.

BASIC: large, thick palm with rough hands and short fingers and nails.

Character: love of out door jobs whereby little mental work is required. Basic living is good enough and no goal to aim for. They have no desire to better themselves and are happy the way they are.

10

SQUARE: square palm with square fingers.

Character: traditionalist yet practical and hard working with an orderly and punctual manner.

SPATULATE: shaped like a spatula with a narrow wrist and widening from the sides of the hand rising upward.

Character: not keen on customs, traditions and repetition and does not care for other's opinions. Yet they are energetic, restless, and irritable, at the same time.

MIXED: consisting of some of the latter hand shapes.

Character: versatile, changeable and sociable, yet they easily become restless and hate to be in the same place for a long time.

FOUR ELEMENTS FOR THE FOUR HAND SHAPES

EARTH - short fingers with square palms: owners of this hand make money slowly through their own perseverance and are thrifty.

AIR - long fingers with square palm: owners of this palm are very up to date with their knowledge on Investments and general financial markets.

FIRE - short fingers with oblong palm: the owners of this palm tend to be more money minded and will not put all their eggs in one basket.

WATER - long fingers with oblong palm: owners of this palm are creative and are not business minded nor materialistic.

THE THUMB

The Thumb is set in opposition to the fingers and helps the rest of the hand to grip and manipulate objects with dexterity and therefore, represents willpower and strength of character.

Thickness of the phalanx (divided sections) describes ones manners - subtle or brusque, pushy or persuasive, self-motivated or relaxed.

Top phalanx represents willpower.

Second phalanx represents one's powers of reasoning.

Pointed thumb - impulsive owner.

Spatulate thumb - owner of this thumb is driven by adventure and excitement (do not confuse this shape with the bulbous thumb tip).

Square thumb - practical logical and law abiding (playing by the rules).

Conic thumb - creative mind.

FINGERS

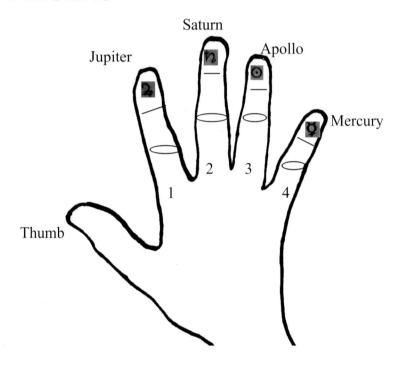

Each finger represents each of personalities:

1st finger - (index) Jupiter: inner confidence, ambition, leadership qualities.

2nd finger - (middle) Saturn: balance of mind, wisdom, responsible, morals.

3rd finger (ring) Apollo: love for art/creativity/acting gambling.

4th finger-(little) Mercury: business acumen, interest in medicine.

MOUNTS

The mounts or the flashy pads represent traits/ facets of our character. If the mounts are flat - it represents lack of that particular emotion and personality and if the mounts are over their size compared to the whole hand it represents overdrive of that emotion and personality.

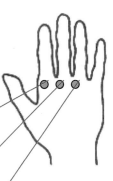

Mount of Jupiter

represents sense of authority self esteem and confidence (longer than other fingers suggests burning ambition and and an overbearing manner.

Mount of Saturn

represents responsibilities (over large reflects a person who is cynical and selfish.

Mount of Apollo

represents creative talent and artistic appreciation.

MOUNTS

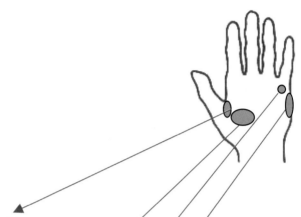

Mars Positive

represents courage, energy, fighting spirit and a sense of self preservation (whereas overlarge represents aggression with cruelty.

Mount of Venus

represents enthusiasm for life, stamina, and vitality.

Mount of Mercury

represents the ability to communicate with others.

Mars Negative

represents staying power and coping under pressure.

MARKINGS FOUND ON THE MOUNTS

Reading a palm is like reading a map, the lines represents the roads, whereas the markings such as star, cross, grille, square, and triangle are like road signs. The signs on the mounts mean the following:

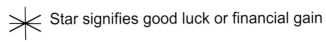 Star signifies good luck or financial gain

— Cross and grille represents negative energies, i.e. opposition

Grille same as above (cross)

— Square signifies protection from full negative energies

△ Triangle indicates success and wisdom

examples: **Star on Mount Mercury** means good fortune. **Grill on Mount Mercury** means unsuccessful business deals. **Triangle on Mount Apollo** success that won't go to your head. **Square on Mount Saturn** means protection from personal or financial loss, however a square on Mount Jupiter signifies gifted teacher/instructor.

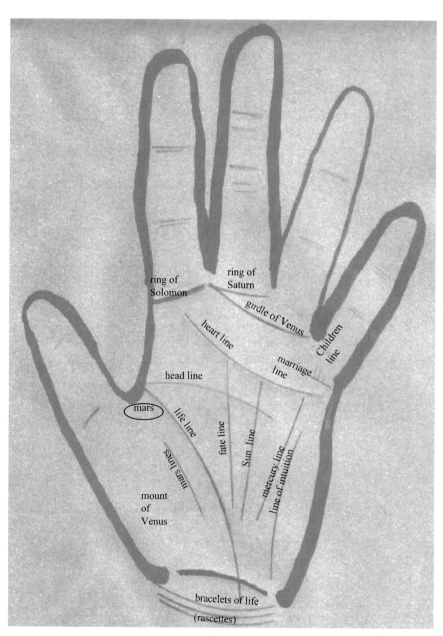

ring of
Solomon

ring of
Saturn

girdle of Venus

heart line

Children
line

head line

marriage
line

mars

life line

fate line

Sun line

mercury line

line of intuition

mars lines

mount
of
Venus

bracelets of life

(rascettes)

MAJOR AND MINOR LINES

LINES

The main lines: the heart, head and life lines are formed in our hands around the 3rd month of foetal development and their construction are determined by our DNA blueprint, therefore any abnormalities during the foetal development will affect the pattern and development of these lines.

The most distinct and deep lines in our palms are decided for us by our genes which are unique symbols of our personal inheritances (i.e. the main lines/fingerprints) and the not so distinct lines are the uninherited, impersonal influences that sometimes arise quite unexpectedly to affect our lives and change accordingly to time and circumstances and therefore, give us an idea of what is to come in our lifetime.

Note: the darker the lines - the more emphasis, energy, and impact, it has on the meaning of the lines.

> *Major lines are already formed during the 3rd month of foetal development*

THE MAJOR LINES

THERE ARE 6 MAIN OR MAJOR LINES ON THE HAND:

HEART LINE: deals with emotions, sentiments and feelings.

HEAD LINE: deals with intelligence, reasoning, practical thinking.

LIFE LINE: deals with health and longevity.

FATE LINE: deals with career and prosperity.

SUN LINE: deals with success, art and a literary career.

MERCURY LINE: deals with business, intelligence and health.

The major lines are already formed in the embryo some time around the third month of development and only the minor lines can and do change according to the individual's surroundings and experiences in life.

THE MINOR LINES

THERE ARE 7 MINOR LINES ON THE HAND:

LINE OF MARS: (this line is inside the life line) which shows good health.

VIA LASCIVA: deals with the lower instincts.

THE GIRDLE OF VENUS: deals with emotions and sexual feelings.

TRAVEL LINE: indicates travel, journey.

LINE OF INTUITION: shows gift of inner-voice.

MARRIAGE LINE: deals with married life.

LINE OF CHILDREN: tells about children in your life.

Please note that minor lines change according to progression and development through life as they are created by our nervous system

THE RASCETTES

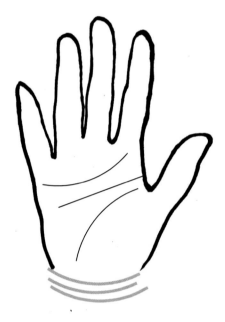

The Rascettes or otherwise known as the bracelets either lined or chained, are usually based nearer to the wrist and are indicators of health, longevity and good luck depending on the colour of these bracelets, and the quantity can be up to four.

If the bracelets are poorly marked then the constitution of the owner is also poor.

Broken or badly formed bracelets indicates trouble.

Chained first bracelet indicates hard labour, will enjoy the fruits at the end.

If the third bracelet is formed with series of small islands – it is an indication of troubled intestines.

MARKINGS FOUND ON THE LINES

Similar to "Markings found on the Mounts" the following are found on the lines:

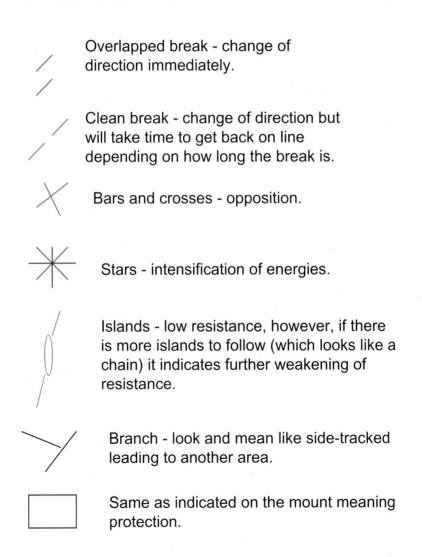

Overlapped break - change of direction immediately.

Clean break - change of direction but will take time to get back on line depending on how long the break is.

Bars and crosses - opposition.

Stars - intensification of energies.

Islands - low resistance, however, if there is more islands to follow (which looks like a chain) it indicates further weakening of resistance.

Branch - look and mean like side-tracked leading to another area.

Same as indicated on the mount meaning protection.

TIMINGS

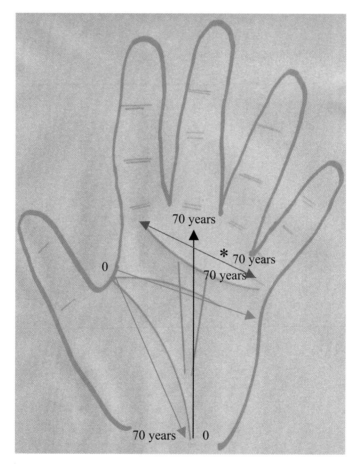

A rough guide to the estimation of the years as per the arrows equals 70 years of age, and the direction that the age is ascending (*however as a point of interest, the Hindus' calculation of the heart line starts from under the mercury finger, others prefer to calculate time from under the index finger).

HAND PRINTS

Being a Palmist myself, it is very important for me to keep records of my clients hand prints and since the minor lines on the hand can change approximately every six months, it updates me on the changes that may have taken place, and the progression of my clients.

Hand prints are invaluable, not only can it be referred to at any time, it also gives a very detailed picture of the smallest markings on the hand which sometimes can be difficult to see especially when the lighting is poor. The only things that cannot be seen of course are the shape and colour of the nails, to which I make my own notes.

Photocopies of the hand is not the best way of reading the hand especially when it comes to reading the minor lines

HOW TO TAKE HAND PRINTS

Fine felt tip pen

ink roller

Water-soluable black ink

A4 plain white paper

Procedures to follow for a good hand print for future reference:

1. Place a small amount of ink onto a flat plastic sheet.

2. Roll the roller over the ink spreading it as evenly as possible leaving the roller without any air bubbles.

3. Start from the base of the palm, slowly rolling upwards and making sure that the ink has spread evenly, repeat this until the whole palm is inked, including the fingers. Then place the inked palm on an A4 sheet (palm first followed by the fingers) adding some body weight to get a good strong print, then slowly move the paper with the hand simultaneously towards the edge of the table or work-top working your way around the corner which in turn will give a good impression of the hollow of the palm. Before the palm is removed from the A4 sheet, draw around the fingers with a fine tip pen. Repeat this performance with the other hand. Take individual finger prints by using an ink pad or again using the inked sheet.

4. Put the name, date of birth, the gender, and date when the hand print was taken and most importantly, whether the person is left handed or right handed.

26

PALMISTRY AND FENG SHUI - THE INTERELATION

We have now gone through the basic knowledge of palmistry, giving an indication of one's character and their future.

As earlier stated, the major lines on our hands are formed in the 3rd month of foetal development, the lines are the inherited genes and therefore, do not change during the course of life. However, the minor lines do change according to one's life experiences and surroundings, which now leads us to the basic knowledge of Feng Shui.

This is where I am inter-relating Feng Shui with Palmistry to create surroundings with positive chi (energy) with harmony and balance, whilst ridding of any negative chi.

FENG
SHUI

WHAT IS
FENG SHUI?

Feng Shui is a Chinese art of placement (pronounced fung shway) meaning wind and water, which was first discovered and implemented by an emperor named Fu His. Feng Shui is a deductive process based on observations of nature, psychology and the immediate surroundings and dates back over 4,000 years ago; it is all about space of a particular person which is a true reflection of one's self, the focus on the individual feel right is of course the emphasis on associations and personal meaning.

Feng Shui is the practice of placing or arranging objects with a particular space so that they are pleasing to you and naturally support you within the context of that space, taking into consideration the conscious and unconscious association you may have with the place and the objects in them, bringing balance and harmony with one's self and their surroundings.

CHI

Chi (pronounced chee) is the universal force of energy or cosmic breath that all things are thought to possess and the movement of Chi is greatly affected by the area through which it flows. Feng Shui in its purest form, simply consists of chi and management, which means keeping the energy moving, not too fast, not too slow. When chi moves too quickly, it invites natural disasters like precipitous slopes that threaten avalanches in the winter, or raging rivers that over flow their banks in the spring. When chi moves too slowly - stagnation results, **e.g**. In a quiet garden fish pond it is thought necessary to add motion by putting fish to simulate chi so that the water would not stagnate and become a breeding place for mosquitoes.

- **(remember every action has a reaction)**

To create harmony and balance, natural forces of positive energy (sheng chi) should be activated to bring in luck, and deactivating any negative chi (shar chi), which only causes bad luck, loss & illness.

YIN YANG

Yin Yang (male & female) symbolises the balance of all aspects of our life as represented in our space. The essence of Feng Shui is to bring harmony and balance within our inner selves as well as our exterior surroundings. **Yin and Yang** are natural forces that are present in all life, continually rising and falling, expanding or withdrawing, and with the state of this dynamic interplay they create the changing pattern of life. Their interaction is clearly seen in the cycle of the seasons. Yang is at its peak in the heat of summer while Yin is at its weakest in winter (as autumn mists appear Yin begins its ascendancy while Yang starts to decline, by midwinter Yang has withdrawn while Yin is powerful, but with the increasing warmth of spring Yang begins to expand once again. e.g. **YANG:** outdoors, bright, hot, fire, day. **YIN:** indoors, dark, cold, water, night.

Too much of Yin or Yang causes imbalance, disharmony and inauspiciousness.

SCHOOLS OF FENG SHUI

Form School where a compass is used known as a **Ba-gua** (which means eight trigrams) divides your house, flat etc...up into 8 areas of enrichments which governs every area of your life, i.e. fame, marriage or commitment, children or creativity, influential people or travel, career, knowledge or spirituality, family and wealth or power according to the directions i.e. south, south west, west etc.....

Compass School follows the form school. It was decided that using a Ba-gua was too subjective and therefore, using various cycles, i.e. year, position, planets and relations of the basic elements by using numerology and astrology was introduced. Further rings were then added to the Ba-gua which comprised multiple sets of rings up to twenty-eight or more information to determine whether amongst other things if your house is right for you. This compass is known as **luo pan** (pronounced low pan).

THE BA-GUA

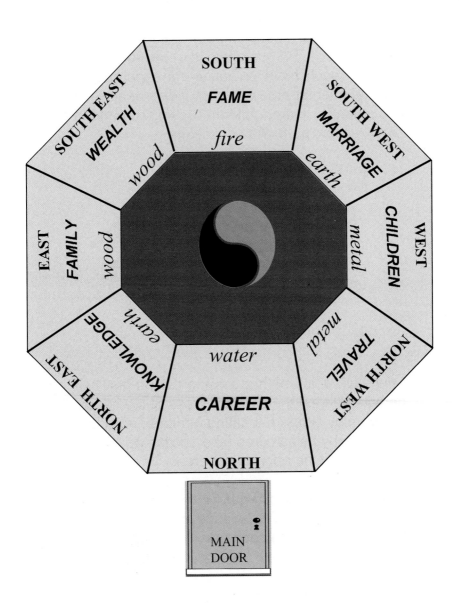

BA-GUA

The **Ba-gua** is a feng shui tool used to analyse and evaluate a room, flat, house or land. **Ba** means eight and **gua** means trigrams thus meaning eight trigrams. The Ba-gua indicates where to find the areas in each room or house corresponding to the eight elemental areas of our lives: wealth, career, relationships, fame, children, travel, knowledge and family according to their directions.

This eight point method - using the Ba-gua helps to detect and treat the problem areas of the house, flat, or room by either re-locating furniture, objects of art, plants, or by using cures (see section on "Cures and Colours") to the appropriate areas.

The centre of the Ba-gua is the Yin Yang symbol which represents the balance of all aspects of our life as represented in our space.

HOW TO USE THE BA-GUA

Following the Black Sect Tantric Buddhist method, we will orient the Ba-gua according to the entrance of each room, or house. The main door of the room is known as the mouth of ch'I.

The first step is to superimpose a copy of the Ba-gua and place it on the floor plan of a room, house or flat. This will enable you to see which corner represents which enrichment.

Secondly, stand in the main entryway or doorway (the mouth of chi) facing inwards towards the room and pointing the south direction of the Ba-gua directly opposite you. The south is the fame area, the corner on the far right becomes the marriage/relation corner, the wall on the right becomes the children/creativity wall, and so on.

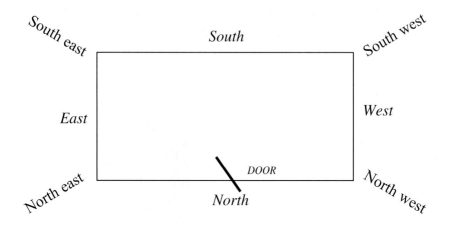

Thirdly, as you can see the room is square/rectangle without any missing corners therefore no missing enrichments.

However, if the area has an irregular shape, extend the lines of its contours until you get a square or rectangle (as below), showing you the missing corner to which the corresponding enrichment is missing and therefore a cure will be required to replenish the missing element.

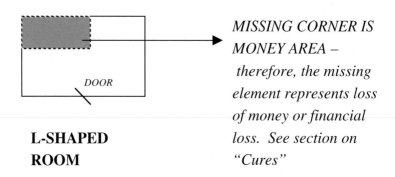

L-SHAPED ROOM

MISSING CORNER IS MONEY AREA –

therefore, the missing element represents loss of money or financial loss. See section on "Cures"

DIRECTIONAL COLOURS

According to Feng Shui all things in the universe belong to one of the following elements and it is vital to balance these elements for harmony : fire, earth, metal, water or wood. But before we examine how the Productive and Destructive cycles work, let us see the examples of objects and colours that represent each of the elements.

South - fire is the element i.e. crystals, light, candles

Colour: red, purple, pink.

South West – earth is the element i.e. earth ware, clay. Colour: yellow.

West - metal is the element i.e.any metal objects

Colour: white, metallic, gold.

North West – metal is the element i.e. any metal objects. Colour: white, grey/ metallic or black.

North - water is the element i.e.stones/pebbles, plants. Colour: black, blue.

North East – earth is the element i.e. earth ware, clay

Colour: black, beige or green.

East - wood is the element i.e. stones, plants, flowers

Colour: green.

South East -wood is the element i.e. stones, plants, flowers. Colour: green.

COLOURS AND CURES

COLOURS ARE VERY GOOD ENHANCERS AND
CURES WHERE NEEDED – PLEASE USE THE
PRODUCTIVE AND DISTRACTIVE CHARTS IN
CONJUNCTION WITH YOUR BA-GUA CHART

red   - strength and romantic energy.

yellow - wealth and power.

Green - growth, health, peace, and future
      prosperity.

Brown - used especially for meditation,
      knowledge, and spirituality.

Pink   - romance, happiness, and love.

Blue   - tranquillity, and career travel.

PRODUCTIVE AND DESTRUCTIVE CYCLE

PRODUCTIVE CYCLE

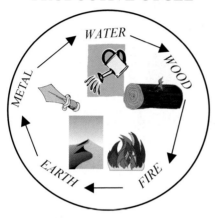

Having found out which element represents what corner, we can now look at how these cycles work and how using this cycle one can increase their enrichments.

Water feeds wood

Wood feeds fire

Fire generates earth

Earth creates metal

Metal holds water

39

DESTRUCTIVE CYCLE

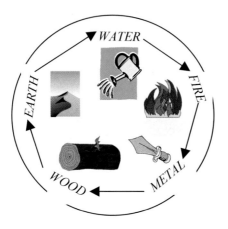

This cycle when used will diminish or destroy the
enrichment.

Water puts out fire

Fire melts metal

Metal cuts wood

Wood breaks up earth

Earth absorbs water

GENERAL TRADITIONAL FENG SHUI CURES

Again using the productive and destructive charts together with the Ba-gua to place the objects in their appropriate corners; using the wrong areas will only counteract the good feng shui.

Mirrors are used for security reasons and to reduce stress by enhancing the cramped surrounds and activates positive chi.

Light focuses on the task ahead and aids in successful finish to a task as well as balances out the yin.

Water Absorbs negative chi and and is a sign of abundance and peace.

Flowers grown in the front of your house signify prosperity, love, health, peace or forgiveness.

Scent used for passion, and helps to keep evil spirits away, i.e. oils, incense sticks.

Crystals signify energy and stability and when placed in front of sunlight, it reflects the healing rainbow of colours.

Wind chimes because of the sound produced when disturbed, it is used as a sign of welcome and helps to circulate chi.

PROBLEMS AND SOLUTIONS:

Q: What can you do if your home is opposite an unwelcoming property i.e. funeral homes, derelict buildings etc..

A: Use of mirrors, lighting, fresh flowers, beautiful peaceful landscapes and paintings, help to activate positive chi into your home. Use curtains or white nets to block the negative chi entering your home.

Q: Lack of concentration at school, work place or studies

A: Mirror helps to cure stress and ones image seen first thing in the morning will give a focus on oneself and in turn give an the impression that builds confidence opening up opportunities and reducing stress.

Q: Lack of bonding with the family/ children

A: Use of the colour green is the bonding colour whereby green represents trees, plants growing and thus building the bond.

Q: Loss of money

A: Check if the bathroom is in the middle of the house, if so this means the prosperity coming into the house is draining out. If the position of the bathroom is unchangeable, use red in colour as red is also the sign to stop.   Always CLOSE THE TOILET LID AFTER EVERY USE as it flushes away prosperity, (so does leaking pipes and taps).

Tips on good Feng Shui

  good flow of chi

 good
lighting

 analyse the
unnecessary
clutter in your home

 Fresh air brings in positive chi
flowing freely around the house
pushing the negative out

mirrors activate
chi

 Fish and water symbolises abundance
of healthy finance

 Wind chimes are used as
a cure when the position
of the desk or bed is not
in view as well as
activate chi

 Plants helps to replace the
negative chi, coming out of
your monitor, with positive chi

Avoid bad feng shui

 blocked flow of chi

Open toilet lid after use

 full dustbins giving off sha chi arrows (poisonous)

clutter

Poor lighting

Leaking taps and pipes puts a drain on your good fortune

Sitting with your back to the door

HOW
PALMISTRY
"Sense"
AND

FENG SHUI
+ *"Visualisation"*

=INTERELATION

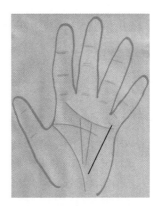

Equilibrium must be present in our body, mind, and spirit to maintain a healthy life which most of us take for granted. This is shown when moons (moons are semi circular usually based on the bottom half of the nail and take approx. 6 months for the nail to grow from bottom to top of the nail), should not be too large. An ideal colour for nails should be pinkie white with no disturbances on the nails,

i.e. white spots,

ridges, brittleness

or with any other

markings.

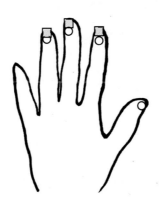

Absence of the mercury line is also a good indication of health.

Health is represented by the yin yang sign in the centre of the Ba gua which means the self and health, and the colour element is yellow.

Crystals are great being placed near the window, letting the sun radiate the rainbow colours to re-energise and to recuperate energy (chandeliers are also used as crystals). Also by decorating the bedroom with vivid and rich hues it gives a feeling of closeness.

Regular flow of fresh air into your home replaces the negative ch'i with positive ch'i .

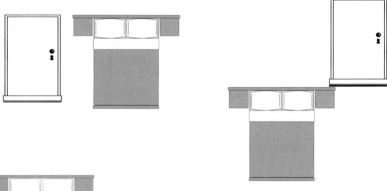

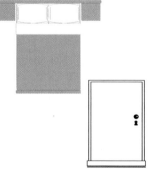

Here are some of the best positions for the bed, try and avoid any overhead beams. If this is not possible use lights/ crystals under the beams as cures for the depressed chi which is acting on the person/s sleeping directly under the beam.

CAREER

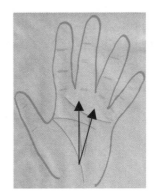

When the presence of the fate is accompanied by the success line then the owner should have no difficulty in reaching their goal in life. Any minor lines shooting off from the fate line or from the life line heading towards any fingers are also success lines (see chapter about "Fingers" and "Minor Lines").

This is where we also look at our working conditions. To help with one's career, one should focus on the sitting position, this can be a start of being comfortable in your work space and any other ventures you want to embark on. Which leads me to the one very common mistake on how the desks should be best positioned.

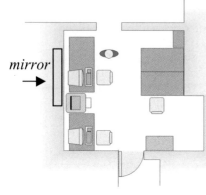

mirror

If it is unavoidable to have your back to the door then place a mirror on the facing wall to avoid any damage to your back when turning to look around. Mirrors are also a good source of using one's reflection to focus on change and as a confidence builder (see section on "Cures").

Since most of us use computers and other machines i.e. printers, photocopiers which churn out negative chi therefore, it helps to place indoor plants near the machines to absorb the negative ch'i.

North Corner is represented by the water element, which includes your current and future profession. The element colour is black which is the conductive colour for success. Using the Ba Gua to see if the corner of career is irregular and if so the colour and water is the element, i.e. water feature water paintings, aquarium with fish are very good sources of inviting good luck in your career.

Using book shelves balances the yin yang in your space.

Red symbolises luck and successes, i.e mouse mat, red flowers etc…

RELATIONSHIPS

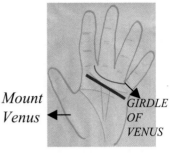

Mount Venus ← *GIRDLE OF VENUS*

Love and relationships are all mirrored in our hands, as well as our attitude towards romance and sexuality. Remember the darker the lines, the more bearing it has on the meanings, and even more so when accompanied by the full Mount of Venus.

For compatibility, hand lines and hand shapes should be compared to decide whether the owner of the hand indicates similar personality and interests (see section on "General Characteristics of the shape of the hand and fingers") bearing in mind the old saying "opposites attract".

***SEXUAL** and sensual overtone are represented by the Girdle of Venus which deals with emotions and sexual feelings; indicated by a line starting between the mount of Jupiter and Saturn and ends in between the mount of Apollo and Mercury. As per latter, presence of a full mount of Venus increases the meaning of the sexual and sensual overtone.*

Early sexual development is indicated by a long Heart line.

Good Feng Shui in the bedroom, use the traditional colour red (universally known for its romantic implications which helps to strengthen the sexual power, fertility and love) i.e. roses, scented candles in the South West (marriage corner).

MARRIAGE/ RELATIONSHIP is represented by the horizontal line/s starting immediately under the mount of Mercury. Love relationships are also indicated by the marriage lines as being a commitment without going through a marriage ceremony or a certificate. Refer to the the "Timings" section to calculate when the events are occurring if any.

Also please see the "Markings on the Lines" for further insight.

CHILDREN lines are the tiny vertical lines on the Mount of Mercury (you may need a magnifying glass and good lighting to see these lines) - refer to the figure on "Major and Minor Lines").

The Corner that deals with Children/Creativity is west and the colour is white although the colour green is a bonding colour together with growth and the element is metal.

PROSPERITY

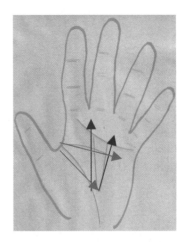

Again prosperity is shown when the fate and success lines are present, however there are other markings to indicate windfalls and inheritances by presences of such markings as:

1) a triangle at the end of the Apollo line;

2) Mercury line showing a good triangle with the joint lines of head line and life line.

3) Apollo line starting from the negative mount of Mars and ending in a trident.

The South East corner represents your financial and influential side of your life. Normally wealth means money or possessions, however, wealth can also mean richness in relationships with family and friends. The element that applies is wind and the colours are blue, purple or red.

PALMISTRY INDEX

PALMISTRY INDEX

FENG SHUI INDEX